Khristian Kritz

the GIFT

Illustrated by
Tahna Desmond Fox

LIONHEART GROUP PUBLISHING
WWW.LIONHEARTGROUPPUBLISHING.COM
PRINTED IN THE USA

The GIFT
Khristian Kritz

This is a work of fiction. Names, characters, places, and incidents are either the product of the author's imagination or, if real, are used fictitiously. Any resemblance to actual persons, living or dead, events, or locales is entirely coincidental.

Lionheart Group Publishing is an independent press, dedicated to publishing timeless books for all ages. Without limiting the rights under copyright reserved below, no part of this publication may be reproduced, stored in or introduced into retrieval system, or transmitted, in any form or by any means (electronic, mechanical, photocopying, recording, or otherwise), including mediums not yet invented, without prior written permission from both the copyright owner and the publisher of this book.

For information regarding reprint or other subsidiary rights, contact Lionheart Group Publishing, attn: permissions department, 1501 Main Street #1023, Canon City, Colorado 81215 or email us at permissions@lionheartgrouppublishing.com

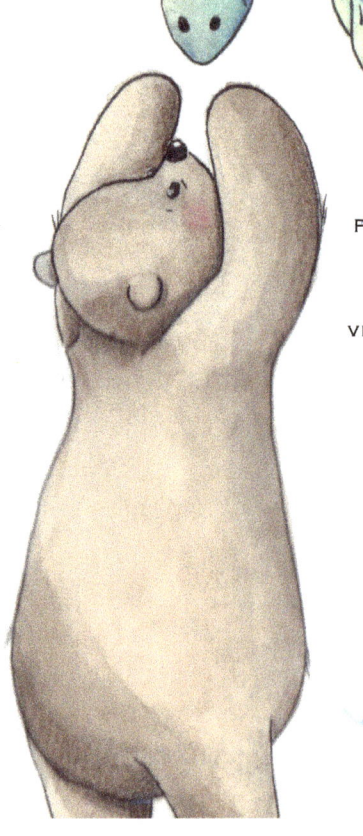

Softcover ISBN: 978-1-938505-51-5
Hardback ISBN: 978-1-938505-50-8
Library of Congress Control Number: 2020930134

Text copyright © 2019 Khristian Kritz
Illustrations copyright © 2019 Tahna Desmond Fox
First Edition ~ January 2020

10 9 8 7 6 5 4 3 2 1

Published by Lionheart Group Publishing, Colorado, USA
Printed in the USA ~ All rights reserved.

visit us on the web at www.lionheartgrouppublishing.com

For Liam Mathieu:

Mathieu means "Gift of God" and you truly have been our gift from God. You have answered so many prayers and brought so much joy and happiness to our lives. Your story is one of great beauty and true love.

~KK

Mama Bear met Papa Bear one beautiful spring day.

They quickly fell deeply in love.

But Mama Bear felt like something was missing. She wanted a baby bear to love and hold.

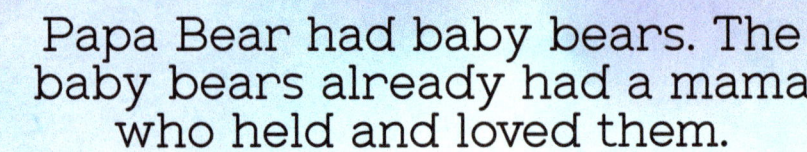

Papa Bear had baby bears. The baby bears already had a mama who held and loved them.

Mama Bear fell down a deep and dark, scary hole.

Papa Bear looked everywhere for Mama Bear, but didn't find her. The hole was too deep and too dark.

Buddy Bear brought Mama Bear food and water.

When she was strong enough, he helped Mama Bear dig herself out of the dark, scary hole.

Buddy Bear stayed by Mama Bear's side while her wounds healed and she grew even stronger. He helped her find her smile.

Even though Buddy Bear was very nice to Mama Bear, the voice in the woods told Mama Bear she was strong enough to go home to Papa Bear.

Buddy Bear sent Mama Bear home with a very special gift.

Khristian Kritz was born in Michigan. She moved to Tennessee as a small child, where she lived until returning to Michigan in 2014 with her husband of ten years, and six-year-old son.

Khristian was a stay-at-home mom for four years while attending Rasmussen College where she received an Associates of Science in Human Services with Honors. She is currently a case manager at Salvation Army, working closely with families in both the Pathways of Hope and Electricity Assistance programs.

Khristian has a strong devotion to meeting the community's needs while spreading hope and grace along the way. While she's mainly worked with the adult population, Khristian's heart truly belongs to helping the younger generation. Her experience has shown her this generation slipped through the cracks of society and could really use a loving hand.

When Khristian is not in the office or with clients, she enjoys cooking, volunteering, and spending time with her family. Her six-year-old son keeps life in perspective and Khristian busy with Cub Scouts and after-school sports.

Tahna Desmond Fox is a formally trained artist who has studied illustration and graphic design for a major portion of her adult life.

While typically a free-lance illustrator, Tahna has also authored two children's books, *My Daddy is a Sailor* and *My Mommy is a Sailor*. Over her ten year career as an graphic artist, Mrs. Fox has had the privilege of illustrating many children's books for other amazing authors. All of which can be found at your favorite online bookstores.

She currently resides wherever the U.S. Navy sees fit, with her sailor husband and two children.

Tahna's family is her inspiration, as she continues on her colorful path of illustration and graphic design, as well as writing.

www.ingramcontent.com/pod-product-compliance
Lightning Source LLC
Chambersburg PA
CBHW042358280426
43661CB00096B/1159